INTRODUCTION
to
ZAMBIAN
ENVIRONMENTAL
LEGISLATIVE SCHEME

CHARLES MWEWA

DEDICATION

For the future of the Republic,
with tremendous concern.

CONTENTS

DEDICATION..iii

CONTENTS..v

BRIEF INTRODUCTION..xi

At the end of the book: xi

Major themes:..xi

FOREWORD xiii

1 | LEGISLATIVE SCHEME 1

2 | ENVIRONMENTAL MANAGEMENT ACT 3

Purpose 3

Divisions of EMA 4

Interpretations...6

    Abatement 6

    Adverse effect 6

    Agency...6

    Appropriate authority 7

    Aquatic environment 7

    Biological diversity 7

    Biological resources..7

    Board...7

    Chairperson 8

    Committee 8

    Compliance order...8

    Conservation 8

Conservancy authority 8

Contaminant 8

Cost order 9

Council 9

Developer 9

Director-General 9

Director of Public Prosecutions 9

Discharge 9

Ecosystem 10

Effect 10

Element 10

Emission 10

Environment 10

Environmental audit 11

Environmental impact assessment 11

Environmental management 11

Environmental management strategy 11

Environmental monitoring 11

Environmental restoration order 12

Extended producer responsibility 12

Exsitu conservation 12

Fund 12

Genetic resources 13

Honorary inspector 13

Insitu conservation 13

Inspector 13

Inspectorate 13

Invasive alien species 13

Noise 14

Occupier 14

Operator 14

Ozone layer 14

Pesticide 14

Policy 15

Pollutant 15

Polluter 16

Polluter pays principle 16

Pollution 16

Precautionary principle 16

Prevention order 17

Private body 17

Proponent 17

Proprietary information 17

Protection order 17

Public body 18

Repealed Act 18

Secretary 18

Segment 18

Sewage 18

Site restoration order 18

Standards 19

Strategic environmental assessment 19

Sustainable development 19

Sustainable use 19

Sustainable management... 19

Toxic substance 20

Vice-chairperson... 20

Waste 20

Wastewater 21

Water 21

Wetland 21

Climate Smart Governance (CSG) Dashboard 22

Superiority of EMA.. 22

Bill of Environmental Rights 22

Environmental Protection as a Duty 22

Twelve Principles of EMA... 23

Forfeiture on Conviction... 24

Section 105 Orders 25

3 | PUBLIC HEALTH ACT 27

Division.. 27

Application 28

Key Environmentally Related Terms 29

Infected 29

Infectious disease... 29

Street.. 30

Premises 30

Public building 30

Public latrine... 30

Sanitary Inspector 30

Drain 31

Dwelling 31

Factory 31

Food 31

Health Inspector 32

Adult 32

Child 32

Board 32

USEFUL WEBSITES 37

ABOUT THE AUTHOR 39

SELECTED BOOKS BY THIS AUTHOR 41

INDEX 47

BRIEF INTRODUCTION

This book introduces the novice concept of environmental protection in Zambia. Zambia, like all countries of the world, is grappling with the vagaries of climate change and global warming. This book considers the major legislative regime that Zambia may rely upon in the interim as it endeavors to legislate further on the environment and the climate.[1]

At the end of the book:

1. You should be able to define Zambia's current legislative regime or scheme on environmental protection and the climate;
2. You should be able to understand the efficacy of the Zambian *Environmental Management Act*; and
3. You should be able to understand the efficacy of the Zambian *Public Health Act*.

Major themes:

1. Legislative regime in Zambia;
2. Review of *Environmental Management Act*; and
3. Review of *Public Health Act*.

---

[1] This book has been reproduced, with necessary modifications, as Chapter 41 in Charles Mwewa, *Zambia: Struggles of My People, 3rd Edition* (Ottawa: ACP, 2024)

The fight for the environment in Zambia is real. Years of negligence can easily turn into environmental disasters for the people. Thankfully, Zambia has a rich legislative scheme which can be the beginning of the journey towards environmental sustainability.

In this book, the author documents the basic legislative scheme that may help in soliciting for tangible future approaches for dealing with environmental protection, climate change and global warming in Zambia.

There are active groups in Zambia such as the Green Cosmos (GRECO), Ecosapentia, and others, that are conscientizing and bringing awareness to the populous.

However, such efforts can go to waste without a strong legislative regime in place. This little book itemizes some notable legislation and regulations that Zambia can make use of in the interim as the battle to protect the environment rages.

Although Zambia has more than two good pieces of legislation on the environment, only two statutes are showcased in this study: The *Environmental Management Act* and the *Public Health Act*. It is the author's belief that these two pieces of legislation provide a formidable introductory and fundamental basis for future enactment of more magnanimous and time-sensitive legislations to effectively combat the whims of environmental degradation, environmental protection, climate change and global warming. The author suggests that this book should be used alongside these two pieces of legislation.

c.m.

FOREWORD

In 2007, the Government of Zambia launched the "Keep Zambia Clean and Health" campaign, which aimed at keeping our surroundings clean to improve the health standard throughout the country. This campaign was a failure from the beginning because it was never implemented. There were many blames heaped on government alone for failed implementation. However, it should be stated that the environment is the responsibility of every citizen, and not of government alone. Keeping Zambia clean must be on every person's mind every day.

Zambia faces a solid waste management strategy problem. Government has not been able to handle it. This has had a devastative impact on the environment. In addition, climate change and global warning have exacerbated the problem. Droughts, floods, and other many effects of climate change have increased in the last five to ten years.

And this is where this book comes in handy. In *Introduction to Zambian Environmental Legislation*, Professor Charles Mwewa has highlighted the key pieces of legislation in Zambia, which, if audaciously implemented, may help to alleviate the adverse effects of climate change and global warming on the Zambian environmental and ecological space. If made to good use, such resources as this, the first one to ever be written about the Zambian environmental legislations, may go a long way to sensitize the population and remind government of its obligation towards implementation.

From my previous experience as an academician, researcher and having graduated with a Bachelor of Arts in Philosophy and Environmental Ethics, I understand that it is everyone's responsibility to protect the environment. And as an environmental activist and Executive Director of Green Cosmos (GRECO), I have had firsthand experience on the importance of encouraging everyone to prioritize the environment. Zambia's unsanitary environment is one of the biggest contributors to climate change. Through our "Keep Zambia Clean" campaigns, we are committed to conscientizing our fellow countrymen and women and to bring awareness to this clear-and-present-danger issue in Zambia.

The Hichilema Government has shown commitment to this issue of the environment by creating the Ministry of Green Economy and the Environment (MGEE). This is a good beginning, and successive governments should emulate this commitment and develop implementable programs to realize the goal. The City of Lusaka has worked with GRECO and other organizations like Ecosapentia in following up on street vending and other environmental concerns. The directorate of the Disaster Management and Mitigation Unity (DMMU) and the Lusaka District Commission have cooperated in keeping Lusaka clean campaigns which in 2023 attracted over 1500 youths to the streets.

Still our streets in Zambia are largely dirty, unsanitary, and prone to outbreaks of diseases like cholera. Statistics regarding the number of people who are concerned about the environmental future of Zambia are dismal, standing at a meagre five percent in 2023. This is very concerning.

However, efforts like what activism is doing, coupled with a resource of this kind, this book, will go a mile further to making Zambia a cleaner and greener space. Professor Mwewa, indeed, should be commended for bringing to Zambia, not only his signature magnum opus, *Zambia: Struggles of My People*, dubbed the "Zambian encyclopaedia;

the Zambian Bible," but, too, this illustrious environmental legal keepsake. I recommend this book to the Government of Zambia, environmental activist groups, environmental NGOs, schools, colleges, and universities, and to the entire Zambian population – because the environment concerns us all.

Thank you, Professor Mwewa, for according to me this rare chance to pen a foreword to this pioneering work, a testament that you have faith in the young people and the future of Zambia.

Martin Mulenga
Executive Director
Green Cosmos (Zambia)

1 | LEGISLATIVE SCHEME

Among the laws, regulations and policies of Zambia dealing with the environment, environmental protection and climate change are the *Public Health Act*, *Extended Producer Responsibility Act*;[2] *Solid Waste Management Act*;[3] and *Local Government Act* of 2011.[4]

Others are the Local Government (Street Vending and Nuisances) (Application);[5] Local Government (Street Vending and Nuisances) (Amendment) Regulations,[6] and the Statutory Instrument on Street Vending; Biotechnology and Biosafety Policy.

Zambia has also enacted the *Environmental Management Act*;[7] and the *Biosafety Act* (which establishes the National Biosafety Authority);[8] and the *Forests Act*.[9]

---

[2] No. 65 of 2018
[3] No. 18 of 2020
[4] Chapter 281 of the Laws of Zambia
[5] Order Chapter 281
[6] Statutory Instrument, No. 10 of 2018
[7] No. 12 of 2011
[8] No. 10 of 2007
[9] No. 4 of 2015

Other statutes on or incidental to the environment in Zambia are the *Zambia Wildlife Act*, 1998; *Water Supply and Sanitation Act*, 1997; *National Heritage Conservation Commission Act; Lands Act; Lands and Deeds Registry Act; Mines and Minerals Development Act*, 2008; and the *Fisheries Act*, 2011.

The *Water Resources Management Act*, 2011; *Inland Waters Shipping Act; Town and Country Planning Act; Standards Act; Disaster Management Act, 2010; Citizens Economic Empowerment Act, 2006; Zambia Development Agency Act, 2006; Public-Private Partnership Act, 2009; Tourism and Hospitality Act, 2007;* and *Energy Regulation Act* form a body of other laws.

2 | ENVIRONMENTAL MANAGEMENT ACT

Purpose

The *Environmental Management Act* ("EMA"):

...provide[s] for integrated environmental management and the protection and conservation of the environment and the sustainable management and use of natural resources; provide[s] for the preparation of the State of the Environment Report, environmental management strategies and other plans for environmental management and sustainable development; provide[s] for the conduct of strategic environmental assessments of proposed policies, plans and programs likely to have an impact on environmental management; provide[s] for the prevention and control of pollution and environmental degradation; provide[s] for public participation in environmental decision-making and access to environmental information; establish the Environment Fund; provide[s] for environmental audit and monitoring; facilitate[s] the implementation of international environmental agreements and conventions to which Zambia is a party;

repeal[s] and replace[s] the *Environmental Protection and Pollution Control Act*, 1990; and provide[s] for matters connected with, or incidental to, the foregoing…[10]

Divisions of EMA

EMA is divided into twelve (12) parts as follows:

Part I – preliminary

Part II – Zambia Environmental Management Agency (ZEMA).
    ZEMA has been empowered by EMA with the power of arrest through its prosecutors.

Part III – integrated environmental management

Part IV – environmental protection and pollution control: This creates eight (8) divisions as follows:

a) pollution control;
b) water;
c) air;
d) waste management;
e) pesticides and toxic substances;
f) noise;
g) ionising radiation; and
h) natural resources management.

Part V – international matters

---

[10] EMA, preamble

Part VI – environmental information

Part VII – public participation

Part VIII – Environmental Fund

Part IX – environmental provisions (such as audits, orders,[11] and civil action).

Part X – rewards and appeals (including right of review; review by the Board; conduct of inquiry; review by the Minister; and appeals).

Part XI – environmental offences.
EMA creates the following seven (7) general offences:
a) Offences relating to environmental impact assessment
b) Offences relating to returns and records
c) Offences relating to environmental standards
d) Offences relating to biological diversity
e) Offences relating to hazardous waste materials, chemicals, and radio-active substances
f) Offences relating to pesticides and toxic substance
g) Offences relating to protected areas

Part XII – general provisions
The general provisions include:
a) Confidentiality
b) General penalty
c) Offence by body corporate or unincorporate body

---

[11] There are several orders including prevention, protection, environmental restoration, compliance, cost and repair, etc.

d) Presumptions
e) Civil damages
f) Forfeiture on conviction
g) Disposal of matter, article, vehicle, aircraft, or boat
h) Power to make orders on process in premises, plant, and machinery
i) Summary imposition of penalties
j) Protected disclosure
k) Regulations

Interpretations

Abatement

Means the reduction, mitigation, or removal of environmental pollution to permitted or prescribed levels;

Adverse effect

Means any harmful or detrimental effect on the environment, whether actual or potential, that—(a) impairs, or may impair, human health; and (b) results in, or may result in, an impairment of the ability of people and communities to provide for their health, safety, cultural and economic wellbeing;

Agency

Means the Zambia Environmental Management Agency provided for under section seven;

Appropriate authority

Means the Minister for the time being having responsibility for, or such public body having powers under any other law over any natural resource, and includes a public or statutory office, body, or institution.

Aquatic environment

Means all surface and ground waters, but does not include water in installations and facilities for industrial effluent, sewage collection and treatment;

Biological diversity

Means the variability among living organisms from all sources including, terrestrial ecosystems, aquatic ecosystems, and the ecological complexes of which they are part, and includes diversity within species, among species, and of ecosystems;

Biological resources

Include genetic resources, organisms, or parts thereof, populations or any other biotiomponent or ecosystems with actual or potential use or value to humanity;

Board

Means the Board of the Agency constituted under section eleven;

Chairperson

Means the person appointed as chairperson of the Board under section eleven;

Committee

Means a committee constituted by the Board under paragraph 2 of the First Schedule;

Compliance order

Means an order issued under section one hundred and six;

Conservation

Means the sustainable management and use of nature and natural resources for their inherent value and for the benefit of human beings and other living things;

Conservancy authority

Means any person or institution who, either voluntarily or under the authority of any law, manages, conserves, preserves, maintains, or protects the environment;

Contaminant

Means a substance, physical agent, energy or a combination of substances and physical agents, that may contribute to, or create a condition of, pollution;

Cost order

Means an order issued under section one hundred and seven;

Council

Means the Environmental Council established under the repealed Act;

Developer

Means a person who proposes to undertake a new project that requires approval under this Act;

Director-General

Means the person appointed as such under section thirteen;

Director of Public Prosecutions

Means the person appointed as such under the constitution;

Discharge

Means spilling, leaking, pumping, pouring, emitting, emptying, or dumping;

Ecosystem

Means a living functional system which contains all organisms including human beings, their environment and the relationship that exists between them;

Effect

In relation to the environment, includes any actual, potential, temporary, permanent, or cumulative effect on the environment;

Element

In relation to the environment, means any of the principal constituent parts of the environment including water, atmosphere, soil, vegetation, climate, sound, odour, aesthetics, fish, and wildlife;

Emission

Means the discharge into the atmosphere of a pollutant from any source in solid, liquid, or gaseous state;

Environment

Means the natural or man-made surroundings at any place, comprising air, water, land, natural resources, animals, buildings, and other constructions;

Environmental audit

Means the systematic, documented, periodic and objective evaluation of how well conservancy authorities and equipment are performing in conserving or preserving the environment;

Environmental impact assessment

Means a systematic examination conducted to determine whether or not an activity or a project has or will have any adverse impacts on the environment;

Environmental management

Means the protection, conservation, and sustainable use of the various elements of the environment;

Environmental management strategy

Means a broad course of action or initiative designed to make the best use of natural resources and opportunities aimed at promoting, protecting, and conserving the environment;

Environmental monitoring

Means the continuous or periodic determination of actual and potential effects of any activity or phenomenon on the environment;

Environmental restoration order

Means an order issued under section one hundred and five;

Extended producer responsibility

Means actions that extend a person's financial or physical responsibility for a product to the post-consumer stage of the product, and includes—

a) waste minimisation programmes;
b) financial contributions to any fund established to promote the minimisation, recovery, reuse, or recycling of waste;
c) awareness programmes to inform the public of the impacts of waste emanating from the product on human health and the environment; and
d) any other measures to reduce the potential impacts of the product on human health and the environment;

Exsitu conservation

Means conservation *outside* the natural ecosystem and habitat of the biological organism;

Fund

Means the Environment Fund established under section ninety-five;

Genetic resources

Means genetic material of actual or potential value;

Honorary inspector

Means any person appointed as such under section seventeen;

Insitu conservation

Means conservation *within* the natural ecosystem and habitat of the biological organisms;

Inspector

Means a person appointed as such under section fourteen;

Inspectorate

Means the inspectorate established under section fourteen;

Invasive alien species

Means an animal or plant with potential to cause harm to the environment when introduced into an ecosystem where the animal or plant does not normally exist;

Noise

Means any undesirable sound that is intrinsically objectionable or that may cause adverse effects on human health or the environment;

Occupier

In relation to any land or premise, means the person in actual occupation of, or in charge of, or responsible for, managing the land or premise;

Operator

In relation to works, industry, undertaking or business, means the person having the control of the works, industry, undertaking or business;

Ozone layer

Means the layer of the atmospheric zone above the planetary boundary layer;

Pesticide

Means any substance or mixture of substances intended for preventing, destroying, or controlling any pest, including vectors of human or animal disease or unwanted species of plants or animals causing harm or otherwise interfering with the production, processing, storage, transport or marketing of food, agricultural commodities, wood, wood products or animal feed, or which may be administered to animals for the control of insects, mites, spider mites or other pests in or on their bodies, and includes substances intended for use as a plant growth regulator, defoliant, desiccant, or agent for thinning fruit or preventing the premature fall of fruit, and substances applied to crops either before or after harvest to protect the commodity from deterioration during storage or transport;

Policy

Plan or program which relates to the whole country, and which is formulated by, or will be implemented by, an organ of Government or a public body, and includes policies, plans and programs relating to national development of urban and rural areas, land use, livestock, transport, the exploitation of minerals, industrial development, water utilisation, agriculture, and any other sector;

Pollutant

Includes any substance whether liquid, solid or gaseous which—

a) may, directly or indirectly, alter the quality of any element of the receiving environment; or
b) is hazardous or potentially hazardous to human health or the environment; and includes objectionable odours, radio-activity, noise, temperature change or physical, chemical, or biological change to any segment or element of the environment;

Polluter

Means a person who contributes to, or creates a condition of, pollution;

Polluter pays principle

Means the principle that the person or institution responsible for pollution or any other damage to the environment shall bear the cost of restoration and cleanup of the affected area to its natural or acceptable state;

Pollution

Means the presence in the environment of one or more contaminants or pollutants in such quantities and under such conditions as may cause discomfort to, or endanger, the health, safety, and welfare of human beings, or which may cause injury or damage to plant or animal life or property, or which may interfere unreasonably with the normal enjoyment of life, the use of property or conduct of business;

Precautionary principle

Means the principle that, lack of scientific certainty should not be used as a reason to postpone measures to prevent environmental degradation, or possible environmental degradation, where there is a threat of serious or irreversible environmental damage, because of the threat;

Prevention order

Means an order issued under section one hundred and three;

Private body

Means any person or organisation which is not a public body, and includes a voluntary organisation, nongovernmental organisation, charitable institution, company, partnership, or a club;

Proponent

Means the government, public body or a corporate body proposing or recommending measures for a policy, program, or plan;

Proprietary information

Means information relating to any manufacturing process, trade secret, trademark, copyright, patent, formula, or other intellectual property protected by law or international treaty to which Zambia is a party;

Protection order

Means an order issued under section one hundred and four;

Public body

Means the government, any Ministry or department of the government, the National Assembly, a local authority, parastatal, board, council, authority, commission, or other body appointed by the government, or established by, or under, any written law;

Repealed Act

Means the *Environmental Protection and Pollution Control Act*;

Secretary

Means the person appointed as such under section thirteen;

Segment

In relation to the environment, means any portion or portions of the environment expressed in terms of volume, space, area, quantity, quality or time or any combination thereof;

Sewage

Means wastewater generated by residential, industrial, and commercial establishments; "sewerage" includes sewage treatment plants;

Site restoration order

Means an order issued under section sixty;

Standards

Means the limits of pollution prescribed under this Act;

Strategic environmental assessment

Means an assessment of the positive and adverse effects or impact that the implementation of a policy, programme or plan has or is likely to have on the protection and conservation of the environment or on the sustainable management of the environment;

Sustainable development

Means development that meets the needs and aspirations of the present generation without causing deterioration or compromising the ability to meet the needs of future generations;

Sustainable use

Means the use of the environment which does not compromise the ability to use the environment by future generations or degrade the capacity of the supporting ecosystems;

Sustainable management

Means protecting and managing the use of the environment, in a manner that, while enabling human beings to provide for their health, safety, social, cultural, and economic well being—

a) safeguards the life-supporting capacity of air, water, soil, and ecosystems;
b) maintains the life-supporting capacity and quality of air, water, soil, and ecosystems, including living organisms, to enable future generations to meet their reasonably foreseeable needs; and
c) avoids the creation of adverse effects, wherever practicable, and where adverse effects cannot be avoided, mitigates, and remedies the adverse effects as far as is practicable;

Toxic substance

Means chemical material, including an object or article, which is poisonous, corrosive, irritant, explosive, inflammable or harmful to human beings, animals, plants, or the environment;

Vice-chairperson

Means the person appointed as vice-chairperson of the Board under section eleven;

Waste

Means any matter whether liquid, solid, gaseous, or radio-active, which is discharged, emitted, or deposited in the environment in such volume, composition, or manner as to cause an adverse effect to the environment, and includes such waste as may be prescribed under this Act;

Wastewater

Means water which has been used for domestic, commercial, agricultural, trading, or industrial purposes and as a result of such use may cause pollution of the aquatic environment when discharged into the aquatic environment;

Water

Means water in its natural state, including—

a) surface water;
b) water which rises naturally on any land or drains or falls naturally on to any land, even if it does not visibly join any watercourse; or
c) ground water;

Wetland

Means a transitional area of marsh, fen, peatland, or water, whether natural or artificial, permanent, or temporary, with water that is static or flowing, fresh, brackish, or salty, including areas of marine water, the depth of which at low tide does not exceed six meters.

Climate Smart Governance (CSG) Dashboard

Is an initiative of the Ministry of Green Economy and Environment (MGEE) which aims at enhancing policy formulation for climate action.

Superiority of EMA

Other than the constitution, EMA is the highest law in Zambia on environmental matters: "Subject to the constitution, where there is any inconsistency between the provisions of this Act and the provisions of any other written law relating to environmental protection and management, which is not a specific subjected related to law on a particular environmental element, the provisions of this Act shall prevail to the extent of the inconsistency."[12]

Bill of Environmental Rights

Other than the constitution, EMA confers rights of clean, safe, and healthy environments in Zambia: "Subject to the Constitution, every person living in Zambia has the right to a clean, safe, and healthy environment."[13]

Environmental Protection as a Duty

Everyone in Zambia has a duty to protect the environment: "Every person has a duty to safeguard and enhance the environment and to inform the Agency of any activity or

---

[12] Section 3
[13] Section 4(1)

phenomenon that affects or may affect the environment." In other words, EMA creates a citizen's arrest provision in environmental matters, a right only conferrable by the *Criminal Procedure Code*.[14]

Twelve Principles of EMA

EMA creates twelve principles on the environment in the quest to achieve EMA's purpose:

a) The environment is the common heritage of present and future generations;
b) Adverse effects shall be prevented and minimized through long-term integrated planning and the co-ordination, integration, and co-operation of efforts, which consider the entire environment as a whole entity;
c) The precautionary principle;
d) The polluter pays principle;
e) Equitable access to environmental resources shall be promoted and the functional integrity of ecosystems shall be taken into account to ensure the sustainability of the ecosystems and to prevent adverse effects;
f) The people shall be involved in the development of policies, plans and programmes for environmental management;
g) The citizen shall have access to environmental information to enable the citizen to make informed personal choices which encourages improved performance by industry and the Government;

---

[14] Chapter 88 of the Laws of Zambia, section 31

h) The generation of waste should be minimised, wherever practicable, and waste should, in order of priority, be re-used, re-cycled, recovered and disposed of safely in a manner that avoids creating adverse effects;

i) The environment is vital to people's livelihood and shall be used sustainably in order to achieve poverty reduction and socio-economic development;

j) Non-renewable natural resources shall be used prudently, taking into account the needs for the present and future generations;

k) Renewable natural resources shall be used in a manner that is sustainable and does not prejudice their viability and integrity; and

l) Community participation and involvement in natural resources management and the sharing of benefits arising from the use of the resources shall be promoted and facilitated

Forfeiture on Conviction

EMA empowers police officers or other peace officers to apply to the court to have an offender's vehicle or vessel to be forfeited to the State: "Subject to the other provisions of this Act, where a person is convicted of an offence under this Act, the court may, on application by an inspector or police officer, in addition to any other penalty imposed, declare any matter, article, vehicle, aircraft, boat, or any other conveyance used in the commission of the offence to be forfeited to the State."[15]

---

[15] Section 129 (1)

Section 105 Orders

These are several orders issued under s. 105 of EMA:

105. (1) An inspector shall, where there is a discharge of a contaminant or pollutant into the environment in an amount, concentration or manner that constitutes a risk to human health or property, or that causes or has the potential to cause adverse effects, serve an **environmental restoration order** on—

a) the owner, manager, or person in control of the premises, vehicle, vessel, aircraft, or equipment from which the discharge was or is being made;

b) any person who, at the time the discharge occurred, was the owner, manager, or person in control of the premises, vehicle, vessel, aircraft, or equipment from which the discharge was made; or

c) any person who caused or permitted the discharge.

(2) An environmental restoration order may require the person on whom it is served to take any measures that will assist in reducing or eliminating the risk or harm and to take any measures to—

a) take such action as will prevent the continuation or cause of pollution;

b) restore land, including the replacement of soil, the replanting of trees and other flora and the restoration as far as may be, of outstanding geological, archaeological, or historical features of the land or the area contiguous to the land or area as may be specified in the particular order;

c) take such action to prevent the commencement or continuation or cause of environmental hazard;

d) cease to take any action which is causing or may contribute to causing pollution or an environmental hazard;

e) remove or alleviate any injury to land or the environment or to the amenities of the area;

f) prevent damage to the land or the environment, aquifers beneath the land and flora and fauna in, on or under or about the land specified in the order or land or the environment contiguous to the land specified in the order;

g) remove any waste or refuse deposited on the land or sea specified in the order and dispose of the same in accordance with the provisions of the order;

h) require the person on whom it has been served to restore the environment as near as it may be to the state in which it was before the asking of the action which is the subject of the order; and

i) prevent the person on whom it is served from taking any action which would or is reasonably likely to cause harm to the environment.

(3) A person on whom an environmental restoration order is served shall comply with the requirements of the order by the date or dates specified in the order and if no date is specified, the person shall comply with the order immediately.

(4) A person who contravenes subsection (4) commits an offence and is liable, upon conviction, to a fine not exceeding three hundred thousand penalty units or to imprisonment for a period not exceeding three years, or to both, and if the person fails to comply with a requirement specified in the order within the specified time, to a further fine not exceeding two thousand penalty units for each day or part of a day after the date specified in the order during which the offence continues.

3 | PUBLIC HEALTH ACT

Purpose:

The purpose of the *Public Health Act*, the ("Act")[16] as stated in the Act, is "to provide for the prevention and suppression of diseases and generally to regulate all matters connected with public health in Zambia."

Division

The Act is divided into fifteen (15) parts, as follows:

Part I – preliminary

Part II – administration (repealed or removed)

Part III – notification of infectious diseases

Part IV – prevention and suppression of infectious diseases

---

[16] Chapter 259 of the Laws of Zambia

Part V – special provisions regarding formidable epidemic disease

Part VI – prevention of the spread of smallpox

Part VII – prevention of introduction of disease

Part VIII – venereal diseases and leprosy

Part IX – sanitation and housing

Part X – protection of foodstuffs

Part XI – water and food supplies

Part XII – prevention and destruction of mosquitoes

Part XIII – cemeteries

Part XIV – General (basements, lodging houses, nursing homes, the Board, control of crops, irrigation, and manufacture of vaccines)

Part XV – miscellaneous provisions (notices, power, and duty of health officers, forms, power of entry, penalties, liabilities of company officers, proceedings against persons, regulations emergency powers, etc.)

Application

The Act applies to apply to anthrax, blackwater fever, epidemic cerebro-spinal meningitis or cerebro-spinal fever, asiatic cholera, diphtheria or membranous croup, dysentery, enteric or typhoid fever (including para-typhoid fever), erysipelas, glanders, leprosy, plague, acute anterior poliomyelitis, puerperal fever (including septicaemia, pyaemia, septic pelvic cellulitis or other serious septic condition occurring during the puerperal state), rabies, relapsing fever, scarlatina or scarlet fever, sleeping sickness or human trypanosomiasis, smallpox or any disease resembling smallpox, typhus fever, all forms of tuberculosis which are clinically recognisable apart from reaction to the tuberculin test, undulant fever and yellow fever.

As *per* section 57, the provisions of this Act do also apply to syphilis, gonorrhea, gonorrhoeal ophthalmia, soft chancre, venereal warts, and venereal granuloma.

The above diseases are known as *notifiable diseases*. In other words, by statutory notice, the Ministry of Health (the "Ministry") may make a declaration that these (or other diseases) are infectious.

Key Environmentally Related Terms

Infected

Means suffering from, or in the incubation stage of, or contaminated with
the infection of, any infectious disease;

Infectious disease

Means any disease (not including any venereal disease except gonorrhoeal ophthalmia) which can be communicated directly or indirectly by any person suffering therefrom to any other person;

Street

Means any highway, road or sanitary lane, or strip of land reserved for a highway, road, or sanitary lane, and includes any bridge, footway, square, court, alley, or passage whether a thoroughfare or not or a part of one;

Premises

Includes any building or tent together with the land on which the same is situated and the adjoining land used in connection therewith, and includes any vehicle, conveyance, or vessel;

Public building

Means a building used or constructed or adapted to be used either ordinarily or occasionally as a place of public worship or as a hospital, college, school, theatre, public hall or as a place of assembly for persons admitted by ticket or otherwise, or used or adapted to be used for any other public purpose;

Public latrine

Means any latrine to which the public are admitted on payment or otherwise;

Sanitary Inspector

Means a Health or Sanitary Inspector in the employment of the Government or of any Local Authority, and includes any person appointed by the Director of Medical Services to act as such within the district of one or more Local Authorities;

Drain

Means any drain used for the drainage of one building only, or of premises within the same curtilage and made merely for the purpose of communicating therefrom with a cesspool or other like receptacle for drainage, or with a sewer, into which the drainage of two or more buildings or premises occupied by different persons is conveyed;

Dwelling

Means any house, room, shed, hut, cave, tent, vehicle, vessel, or boat or any other structure or place whatsoever, any portion whereof is used by any human being for sleeping or in which any human being dwells;

Factory

Means any building or part of a building in which machinery is worked by steam, water, electricity, or other mechanical power, for the purposes of trade;

Food

Means any article used for food or drink other than drugs or water, and any article intended to enter into or be used in the preparation of such food, and flavouring matters and condiments;

Health Inspector

Means a Health or Sanitary Inspector in the employment of the Government or of any Local Authority, and includes any person appointed by the Director of Medical Services to act as such within the district of one or more Local Authorities;

Adult

Means a person who is over or appears to be *over eighteen years of age*;

Child

Means a person who is under or appears to be *under eighteen years of age*;

Board

Means the *Central Board of Health* constituted under this Act.

The Ministry is responsible for delegating to the Local Authority the authority and duty to clean and disinfect premises.[17] A medical officer is, thus, by the authority given to them, empowered to enter a premise any time and to inspect it.

The Minister of Health is empowered by the Act to enact regulations dealing with infectious diseases.[18] These regulations, without limiting their generality, do also apply to epidemics.[19]

---

[17] Section 16
[18] Section 28
[19] Section 29

Similarly, the Minister may prevent any immigrant from entering Zambia if suspected of any infectious disease.[20]

Part IX of the Act deals with sanitation, which is quintessentially an environmental issue. The Act empowers Local Authorities to prevent or remedy dangers to health arising from unsuitable dwellings.[21]

Nuisance is addressed in the Act.[22] It is defined as any vessel or any railway carriage, any dwelling or premises or part thereof, any street, road or part thereof, other source of water supply or any cistern or other receptable, any noxious matter, or wastewater, flowing or discharged from any premises, any stable, cow-shed or other building or premises used for keeping of animals or birds, any animal so kept as to be a nuisance, or injurious to health, any offensively accumulation or deposit of refuse, offal, manure or other matter, smoke chimney, cemetery or burial place, etc.

The person who perpetuates or releases such nuisance is called an *author of the nuisance.*

Penalties for failure to comply with an order to remove a nuisance is

> ...a fine not exceeding one hundred and twenty penalty units for every day during which the default continues; any person wilfully acting in contravention of a closing order issued under the last preceding section shall be liable to a fine not exceeding one hundred and twenty penalty units for every day during which the contravention continues.[23]

---

[20] Section 49
[21] Section 66
[22] Section 67
[23] Section 70

It must be noted that the penalty increases as the order continues to be disobeyed.

Foodstuffs must be kept in rat-free storages.[24] And the Act prevents any person to reside or sleep in any room in which foodstuffs are stored, etc.[25]

Local Authorities must "take all lawful, necessary and reasonably practicable measures" to prevent water pollution and what the Act terms as *unwholesome food*.[26]

The Minister must appoint cemeteries in "proper places."[27] However, only a magistrate may make an order for exhumation.[28]

The Minister may direct that a covering over graves be removed for public, industrial or mining purposes.[29] The Minister has a residual authority to close certain cemeteries.[30]

The Local Authority may apply to the Minister to have additional public localities to be designated for latrine accommodation.[31]

In certain circumstances, the Act gives the Local Authority emergency powers:

> Where in any district no Medical Officer of Health is immediately available and where the circumstances render immediate action necessary for the prevention of the spread of disease or generally for safeguarding the health and well-being of the community, the Local Authority may exercise the powers conferred and

---

[24] Section 76
[25] Section 77
[26] Sections 78-81
[27] Section 91
[28] Section 93(4)
[29] Section 94
[30] Section 96
[31] Section 101

perform the duties imposed by this Act on a Medical Officer of Health.[32]

Thus, the Act empowers the Local Authority to implement emergency measures when the presence of a Medical Officer of Health is required but cannot be accessed.

---

[32] Section 116

USEFUL WEBSITES

Ministry of Green Economy and Environment -
https://www.mgee.gov.zm/#

Ecolex - https://www.ecolex.org/details/legislation/local-government-street-vending-and-nuisances-no-2-regulations-cap-281-lex-faoc092651/

Ecosapentia Zambia - https://ecosapentia.com/

Green Cosmos Zambia - https://www.greencosmoszambia.org/

Public Health Act Zambian Parliament -
https://www.parliament.gov.zm/sites/default/files/documents/acts/Public%20Health%20Act.pdf

World Vision Zambia -
https://www.wvi.org/stories/zambia/trees-are-our-lifeline

WWF Zambia - https://www.wwfzm.panda.org/

ZEMA - https://www.zema.org.zm/

ZEM Zambian Parliament -
https://www.parliament.gov.zm/sites/default/files/documents/acts/Environmetal%20Mangement%20Act%2012%20of%202011.pdf

ABOUT THE AUTHOR

Best Selling Author, Charles Mwewa (LLB; BA Law; BA Ed; LLM), is a prolific researcher, poet, novelist, lawyer, law professor and Christian apologist and intercessor. Mwewa has written no less than 90 books and counting in every genre and has exhibited his works at prestigious expos like the Ottawa International Book Expo and is the winner of the Coppa Awards for his signature publication, *Zambia: Struggles of My People.*
Mwewa and his family live in the Canadian Capital City of Ottawa.

SELECTED BOOKS BY THIS AUTHOR

1. *ZAMBIA: Struggles of My People (First and Second Editions)*
2. *10 FINANCIAL & WEALTH ATTITUDES TO AVOID*
3. *10 STRATEGIES TO DEFEAT STRESS AND DEPRESSION: Creating an Internal Safeguard against Stress and Depression*
4. *100+ REASONS TO READ BOOKS*
5. *A CASE FOR AFRICA?S LIBERTY: The Synergistic Transformation of Africa and the West into First-World Partnerships*
6. *A PANDEMIC POETRY, COVID-19*
7. *ALLERGIC TO CORRUPTION: The Legacy of President Michael Sata of Zambia*
8. *BOOK ABOUT SOMETHING: On Ultimate Purpose*
9. *CAMPAIGN FOR AFRICA: A Provocative Crusade for the Economic and Humanitarian Decolonization of Africa*
10. *CHAMPIONS: Application of Common Sense and Biblical Motifs to Succeed in Both Worlds*
11. *CORONAVIRUS PRAYERS*
12. *HH IS THE RIGHT MAN FOR ZAMBIA: And Other Acclaimed Articles on Zambia and Africa*
13. *I BOW: 3500 Prayer Lines of Inspiration & Intercession from the Heart: Volume One*
14. *INTERUNIVERSALISM IN A NUTSHELL: For Iranian Refugee Claimants*
15. *LAW & GRACE: An Expository Study in the Rudiments of Sin and Truth*
16. *LAWS OF INFLUENCE: 7even Lessons in Transformational Leadership*
17. *LOVE IDEAS IN COVID PANDEMIC TIMES:*

For Couples & Lovers

18. *P.A.S.S: Version 2: Answer Bank*
19. *P.A.S.S.: Acing the Ontario Paralegal-Licensing Examination, Version 2*
20. *POETRY: The Best of Charles Mwewa*
21. *QUOT-EBOS: Essential. Barbs. Opinions. Sayings*
22. *REASONING WITH GOD IN PRAYER: Poetic Verses for Peace & Unconfronted Controversies*
23. *RESURRECTION: (A Spy in Hell Novel)*
24. *I DREAM OF AFRICA: Poetry of Post-Independence Africa, the Case of Zambia*
25. *SERMONS: Application of Legal Principles and Procedures in the Life and Ministry of Christ*
26. *SONG OF AN ALIEN: Over 130 Poems of Love, Romance, Passion, Politics, and Life in its Complexity*
27. *TEMPORARY RESIDENCE APPLICATION*
28. *THE GRACE DEVOTIONAL: Fifty-two Happy Weeks with God*
29. *THE SYSTEM: How Society Defines & Confines Us: A Worksheet*
30. *FAIRER THAN GRACE: My Deepest for His Highest*
31. *WEALTH THINKING: And the Concept of Capisolism*
32. *PRAYER: All Prayer Makes All Things Possible*
33. *PRAYER: All Prayer Makes All Things Possible, Answers*
34. *PRISONER OF GRACE: An I Saw Jesus at Milton Vision*
35. *PRAYERS OF OUR CHILDREN*
36. *TEN BASIC LESSONS IN PRAYER*
37. *VALLEY OF ROSES: City Called Beautiful*
38. *THE PATCH THEOREM: A Philosophy of Death, Life and Time*
39. *50 RULES OF POLITICS: A Rule Guide on Politics*
40. *ALLERGIC TO CORRUPTION: The Legacy of*

President Michael Sata of Zambia

41. *INTRODUCTION TO ZAMBIAN ENVIRONMENTAL LEGISLATIVE SCHEME*

42. *REFUGEE PROTECTION IN CANADA: For Iranian Christian Convert Claimants*

43. *CREDIBILITY: Nigerian Refugee Claims in Canada*

44. *LAW & POVERTY (unpublished manuscript)*

45. *CHRISTIAN CONTROVERSIES: Loving Homosexuals*

46. *THINKING GOVERNMENT: Principles & Predilections*

47. *WHY MARRIED COUPLES LIE TO EACH OTHER: A Treatise*

48. *LOVE & FRIENDSHIP TIPS FOR GEN Z*

49. *POVERTY DISCOURSE: Spiritual Imperative or Social Construct*

50. *SEX BEFORE WEDDING: The Tricky Trilemma*

51. *QUOTABLE QUOTES EXCELLENCE, VOL. 1: Knowledge & Secrets*

52. *QUOTABLE QUOTES EXCELLENCE, VOL. 2: Love & Relationships*

53. *QUOTABLE QUOTES EXCELLENCE, VOL. 3: Hope*

54. *QUOTABLE QUOTES EXCELLENCE, VOL. 4: Justice, Law & Morality*

55. *QUOTABLE QUOTES EXCELLENCE, VOL. 5: Dreams & Vision*

56. *QUOTABLE QUOTES EXCELLENCE, VOL. 6: Character & Perseverance*

57. *QUOTABLE QUOTES EXCELLENCE, VOL. 7: Actions*

58. *QUOTABLE QUOTES EXCELLENCE, 1 of 20: Knowledge & Secrets*

59. *QUOTABLE QUOTES EXCELLENCE, 2 of 20: Love & Relationships*

60. *QUOTABLE QUOTES EXCELLENCE, 3 of 20:*

Hope

61. *QUOTABLE QUOTES EXCELLENCE, 4 of 20: Justice, Law & Morality*
62. *QUOTABLE QUOTES EXCELLENCE, 5 of 20: Vision & Dreams*
63. *THE SEVEN LAWS OF LOVE*
64. *THE BURDEN OF ZAMBIA*
65. *BEMBA DYNASTY I (1 of a Trilogy)*
66. *BEMBA DYNASTY II (2 of a Trilogy)*
67. *ETHICAL MENTORSHIP: Missing Link in Transformational Leadership*
68. *AFRICA MUST BE DEVELOPED: Agenda for the 22nd Century Domination*
69. *INNOVATION: The Art of Starting Something New*
70. *TOWARDS TRUE ACHIEVEMENT: The Mundane & the Authentic*
71. *ONE WORLD UNDER PRAYER: For Camerron, Ecuador, and France*
72. *ONE WORLD UNDER PRAYER: For New Zealand, Poland, and Uganda*
73. *ONE WORLD UNDER PRAYER: For Malta, USA, and Zambia*
74. *ONE WORLD UNDER PRAYER: For Germany*
75. *ONE WORLD UNDER PRAYER: For Haiti, Iraq, and Russia*
76. *ONE WORLD UNDER PRAYER: For Chad, UN, and Syria*
77. *ONE WORLD UNDER PRAYER: For Burundi, Canada, and Israel*
78. *ONE WORLD UNDER PRAYER: For China, Egypt, and Venezuela*
79. *ONE WORLD UNDER PRAYER: For Greece, Mali, and Ukraine*
80. *ONE WORLD UNDER PRAYER: For Morocco,*

North Korea, and the UK

81.   ONE WORLD UNDER PRAYER: For Belgium, Brazil, and the Burkina Faso

82.   ADIEU PERFECTIONS: A Satire

83.   OPTIMIZATION: Turning Low Moments into High Comments

84.   ACING THE IMPOSSIBLE: Faith in the Other Dimension

85.   END GAME LAW: Financial Mindset in Quotables

86.   THE RULE MODERATION THEOREM OF GOVERNANCE: An Introduction

INDEX

A

Abatement, 6
Adult, 32
Adverse effect, 6
Africa, 41, 42
Agency, 6
aircraft, 6, 24
anthrax, 28
Appropriate authority, 7
Aquatic environment, 7
asiatic cholera, 28
audits, 5

B

basements, 28
Biological diversity, 7
Biological resources, 7
Biosafety Act, 1
Biotechnology and Biosafety Policy, 1
blackwater fever, 28
Board, 7
boat, 6, 24, 31

C

Capisolism, 42
cerebro-spinal fever, 28
Chairperson, 8
Child, 32
Christian, 39
Citizens Economic Empowerment Act, 2
civil action, 5
Civil damages, 6
clean, safe, and healthy environments, 22
Climate Smart Governance (CSG)

Dashboard, 22
Committee, 8
Compliance order, 8
Confidentiality, 5
Conservancy authority, 8
Conservation, 2, 8
constitution, 9, 22
Contaminant, 8
corporate, 5
Cost order, 9
crops, 15, 28

D

Developer, 9
diphtheria or membranous croup, 28
Director of Public Prosecutions, 9
Director-General, 9
Disaster Management Act, 2
Disaster Management and Mitigation
    Unity (DMMU), xiv
Discharge, 9
diseases, 27, 28, 29, 32
Drain, 31
droughts, xiii
Dwelling, 31
dysentery, 28

E

Ecosapentia, xiv, *See* environment
Ecosystem, 10
Effect, 10
emergency powers, 28, 34
Emission, 10
Energy Regulation Act, 2
environment, xii
Environment, 10

Environment Fund, **3, 12**
Environmental audit, **11**
Environmental impact assessment, **11**
environmental management, **3, 4, 23**
Environmental management, **11**
Environmental Management Act, **xii, 1, 3**
Environmental management strategy,
  11
Environmental monitoring, **11**
environmental offences, **5**
*Environmental Protection and Pollution
  Control Act*, **4**
Environmental restoration order, **12**
epidemic cerebro-spinal meningitis, **28**
erysipelas, **29**
Exsitu conservation, **12**
Extended producer responsibility, **12**
Extended Producer Responsibility Act, **1**

F

Factory, **31**
fever, **29**
Fisheries Act, **2**
floods, **xiii**
Food, **31**
foodstuffs, **28, 34**
Forests Act, **1**
Forfeiture on conviction, **6**
Fund, **12**

G

General penalty, **5**
Genetic resources, **13**
glanders, **29**
global warming. *See* **environment**
God, **42**
gonorrhea, **29**
Green Cosmos. *See* **environment**
Green Cosmos (GRECO), **xiv**

H

Health Inspector, **32**
health officers, **28**
Hichilema Government, **xiv**
Honorary inspector, **13**
human trypanosomiasis, **29**

I

implementation, **xiii, 3, 19**
Infected, **29**
Infectious disease, **29**
Inland Waters Shipping Act, **2**
Insitu conservation, **13**
Inspector, **13**
Inspectorate, **13**
Invasive alien species, **13**
ionising radiation, **4**

K

Keep Zambia Clean, **xiii, xiv**
Keep Zambia Clean and Health, **xiii**

L

Lands Act, **2**
Lands and Deeds Registry Act, **2**
law, **39**
laws, **1**
lawyer, **39**
leprosy, **28, 29**
liabilities, **28**
Local Government (Street Vending and
  Nuisances), **1**
Local Government Act, **1**
lodging houses, **28**
Lusaka District Commission, **xiv**

M

machinery, 6, 31
Medical Officer of Health, 34
Mines and Minerals Development Act, 2
Ministry of Green Economy and
    Environment, 37
Ministry of Health, 29
mosquitoes, 28

N

National Biosafety Authority. *See*
    Biosafety Act
*National Heritage Conservation Commission
    Act;*, 2
natural resources management, 4, 24
NGOs, xv
noise, 4
Noise, 14
nursing homes, 28

O

Occupier, 14
Operator, 14
Ozone layer, 14

P

penalties, 6, 28
Pesticide, 14
pesticides and toxic substances, 4
plague, 29
Policy, 15
Pollutant, 15
Polluter, 16
Polluter pays principle, 16
Pollution, 16
pollution control, 4
Precautionary principle, 16

Premises, 30
Presumptions, 6
Prevention order, 17
Private body, 17
professor, 39
Professor Charles Mwewa, xiii
Professor Mwewa. *See* Professor
    Charles Mwewa
Proponent, 17
Proprietary information, 17
Protected disclosure, 6
Protection order, 17
Public body, 18
Public building, 30
Public Health Act, xii, 1, 27, 37
Public latrine, 30
Public-Private Partnership Act, 2

R

rabies, 29
Regulations, 1, 6
Repealed Act, 18

S

Sanitary Inspector, 30
sanitation, 28, 33
Secretary, 18
Section 105 Orders, 25
Segment, 18
Sewage, 18
Site restoration order, 18
smallpox, 28, 29
Solid Waste Management Act;, 1
solid waste management strategy, xiii
Standards, 19
Standards Act, 2
State of the Environment Report, 3
Statutory Instrument on Street Vending,
    1
Strategic environmental assessment,

19
Street, 30
Struggles of My People, **39**, **41**
Sustainable development, **19**
sustainable management, **3**
Sustainable management, **19**
Sustainable use, **19**
syphilis, **29**

T

the West, **41**
Tourism and Hospitality Act, **2**
Town and Country Planning Act, **2**
Toxic substance, **20**
tuberculin, **29**
twelve principles, **23**
typhoid, **29**
typhus, **29**

U

unincorporate, **5**

V

vaccines, **28**
venereal granuloma, **29**
venereal warts, **29**
Vice-chairperson, **20**

W

Waste, **20**
waste management, **4**
Wastewater, **21**
Water, **21**
Water Resources Management Act, **2**
Water Supply and Sanitation Act, **2**
Wetland, **21**
World Vision Zambia, **37**
WWF Zambia, **37**

Y

yellow fever, **29**

Z

Zambia, **39**, **41**, **42**, **43**
Zambia Development Agency Act, **2**
Zambia Environmental Management
    Agency (ZEMA), **4**
Zambia Wildlife Act, **2**
Zambia: Struggles of My People, **xiv**
Zambian Bible. *See* **Zambia: Struggles
    of My People**
Zambian encyclopaedia. *See* **Zambia:
    Struggles of My People**

www.ingramcontent.com/pod-product-compliance
Lightning Source LLC
Chambersburg PA
CBHW070826210326
41520CB00011B/2139